LET'S GO to build the first
TRANSCONTINENTAL RAILROAD

LET'S GO to build the first

TRANSCONTINENTAL
RAILROAD

by Bernard Rosenfield

Illustrated by Albert Micale

G. P. PUTNAM'S SONS   NEW YORK

Second Impression

All rights reserved
Published simultaneously in the Dominion of Canada by
Longmans Canada Limited, Toronto
Library of Congress Catalog Card Number: 63-7753
MANUFACTURED IN THE UNITED STATES OF AMERICA

You are a boy of thirteen who has just taken a job with the Union Pacific Railroad to build part of the transcontinental railroad. It is the year 1868 and you are on a train hurtling to "end o' track," the farthest point to which the Union Pacific has laid rails.

Where is end o' track now? How far has it reached? The last you heard, it was at Sherman Summit, Wyoming, 540 miles from Omaha, Nebraska, the starting point. Meanwhile, the Central Pacific Railroad is building somewhere in Nevada, racing to meet the Union Pacific.

All the people on the train share your excitement. There are other men and boys who also have jobs. There are passengers for different stops along the way. People are going by train to stations that did not even exist a few weeks ago! Some are tourists going to visit end o' track and watch the construction. Others are immigrants going west to start new homes.

Conversation is lively. You talk of places you have already passed. Omaha, North Platte, and Julesburg once seemed as far away to you as the moon. Now you have actually seen them.

You look out the window at the rolling prairie. As far as the eye can see there is flat, treeless country. Off in the distance you see a herd of buffalo, stirring up a great cloud of dust as it disappears off in the distance, frightened by the noise of the train.

Someone tells you that the buffalo used to get in the way of the builders. But now that the Union Pacific has built across Nebraska, the buffalo have learned to fear the trains. This has caused even greater troubles.

The Indians who live here depend upon these animals. Now they are beginning to roam far from the tracks. The Indians are go-

ing hungry, and this great railroad is threatening their very existence.

As a result, the Indians are trying their best to stop the trains. Stations have been attacked. Workers have been killed. Trains have been ambushed and burned. The danger is so great that the United States Army has been summoned to protect the trains and builders.

Suddenly you are jolted by the loud blast of the train whistle. Off in the distance you hear another train whistle. You realize that you are approaching a train heading east on the same track. How will it pass? This is only one track.

You don't have long to wonder. Your train soon begins to slow down, and then with a lurch it is switched to another track which runs alongside the main track. This is one of the many "sidings" which are built about every 15 miles along the route to permit trains to pass each other.

The eastbound train whistles by on the main track with a roar. The passengers from the two trains wave at each other, and soon the

other train is gone. Your train starts up slowly, switches back to the main track, and is soon speeding along as before.

Now you are approaching Cheyenne, "Magic City of the Plains." Here, at this outpost in the West, you will learn exactly what your duties will be and where you will be sent.

The train pulls slowly into Cheyenne, a strange frontier town like none you have ever seen before. Everywhere you see tents, shacks, and log cabins. Everything seems built in a hurry, and nothing looks as if it could last very long.

As you get off the train, you are directed to the headquarters building a short distance away. There are no paved streets in Cheyenne, and you pick your way through mud and dirt and wagon wheel ruts.

Most of the people you pass are men and they look as rough as their surroundings. You notice that the largest tents and log cabins are saloons and dance halls.

Suddenly you hear gun shots, and along with everyone else, you run for cover. Two men have had an argument and are shooting it out. From your hiding place you see one of the men fall. The winner replaces his revolver in its holster, and calmly walks away. People come out of hiding as if nothing has happened. But where are the police, you wonder? Then

you realize you are not back East where there is law and order. Cheyenne is a brand new town that grew up almost overnight. This is indeed the Wild West! It is easy to see why this town is called "Hell on Wheels."

When you report to headquarters, you are told that you will be a water boy for the construction men. The track, you learn, has crossed the Laramie Mountains, and is a few miles from the town of Laramie, where you will join the crew.

You return to the station, eager for the adventure that lies ahead. You board a construction train much different from the one that brought you to Cheyenne. This one carries work crews, stacks of rails, ties, spikes, tools and other materials.

Soon you are under way, speeding westward. You pass other trains on sidings, some loaded with supplies, waiting their turn to head for end o' track. Others are empty and soon will head east for another load.

The foreman of your crew tells you about the tremendous job of providing materials for the construction men. It takes 40 carloads of supplies to build a single mile of track! And all of this material is manufactured in the East. It is sent to the Mississippi River and from there up the Missouri River by boat. From Omaha, every bit of it has to be carried on the part of the railroad which has already been built.

But this past winter the men were able to obtain some of the supplies near end o' track. For the first time, in the Laramie Mountains, the railroad was near trees. When construction stopped for the winter the men used the time to cut "ties," the wooden supports to which the rails are fastened.

The train reaches the Laramie Mountains and starts to climb. It heaves and it puffs as it pulls its heavy load up the steep grade. Soon you are at the top and the foreman tells you that you are 8000 feet up, the highest point that the Union Pacific will cross. Soon you start down the other side and continue on your way.

"There it is!" shouts the foreman. The train slackens its speed and stops at end o' track.

Immediately men are swarming over the train and unloading the supplies. Everything

is hurriedly thrown to the ground on either side. The men work so quickly that you have barely enough time to get out of their way.

Before you know it, everything is unloaded. The empty train then moves backward toward Cheyenne. Soon it is gone.

Immediately another train arrives from the direction of end o' track. It is different from any train you have ever seen. This is the "boarding train." There are cars for sleeping and for eating. One is a cookhouse. You see an office, a general store and a saloon. The boarding train moves beyond the pile of supplies.

Fascinated, you watch another strange sight. Following the boarding train comes a small, horse-drawn car, which stops right at the supplies. Immediately men start loading the material.

You see them lift sections of iron rail, each about 28 feet long. It takes many men to do the job, for each piece weighs about 350 pounds. You see them load "chairs," which are the iron supports that are set on the ties and hold the rails in place. You see them load "spikes," the long iron nails which are driven into the ties to fasten the chairs and the rails. Soon the car is loaded, and you follow it as the horses draw it westward.

Now at last you see it, the exact spot where the rails end! There is a bustle of frantic activity. As the car reaches end o' track, checks are placed under the wheel to stop it, and the horses are unhitched.

Almost before the car stops, six men take their places on either side of it. They pull two sections of rail off the car and put them on rollers. The men push the rails forward, and then pick them up to hold them in place over the ties.

"Ready! Down!" comes the command of the chief, and the rails are dropped with a deafening clang onto the chairs that have already been placed on the ties. Other men "gauge" the rails, to make sure they are straight and the correct distance apart.

Next the car is pushed over the loose rails to the new end o' track, and the operation is repeated. Every time two new rails are laid, the railroad moves 28 feet closer to the Pacific Ocean!

Then you see other men follow and put spikes into place. Still others follow them and drive the spikes into the ties with heavy sledgehammers. They stamp the earth under the ties, and the new section of railroad is complete.

18

The track surges forward so quickly that you must keep moving with the car or you will be left behind. Suddenly you hear a warning shout to get out of the way. You jump aside as you see the empty car being tipped over and thrown from the tracks to make way for a fully loaded one. When the full car passes, the empty car is returned to the tracks and is pulled back to the supplies for another load.

Before long you start work. Back and forth you go with your bucket, between the water supply and the work crew. Other boys your

age are also carrying water. That night, weary from work and the excitement of your first day, you are glad to have dinner and sleep on the boarding train.

The next day is the same as the first. And so it continues, day after day, rail after rail, mile after mile, as the tracks move ever westward.

At the end of April startling news reaches end o' track. The Central Pacific is building faster than expected, and the main office of the Union Pacific in New York has issued new orders. Seven hundred miles of track must be laid in the next four months, a distance that would take eight months at the present rate. The race with the Central Pacific gains new fury as everyone agrees to increase his efforts and speed up the work.

That afternoon you are called to the office in the boarding car and asked if you know how to ride a horse and handle a rifle. When you say yes, you are given the exciting news that you and one of the men will leave immediately on a special mission.

You are being sent ahead as messengers to bring the news of the speed-up to the graders, engineers and surveying parties. Some of them may be more than 100 miles away. They, too, must increase their rate of work. The two of you will travel through hostile Indian country to reach the most advanced party of surveyors. It will be a difficult trip. Speed is important, and you cannot take much with you. You will have your rifles which will be not only for protection. You will also use them to shoot game for food.

Soon you are on your way. About two miles beyond end o' track you overtake the tie men who lay the wooden ties on the road bed. The

construction crews that follow lay the rails onto these ties. Even though they are only two miles ahead of the others, these men are in constant danger from Indian attack, because there are just a few of them. You see neat stacks of rifles within easy reach.

It is not difficult to follow the route of the railroad. Stretching before you is the road bed which has been prepared by the graders. It is level and smooth, and ready for the ties and rails that will follow.

Your journey continues, and you cross the newly constructed bridges over the Laramie and Medicine Bow Rivers. Later on, when you reach the North Platte River, you see the construction men still at work on the incomplete bridge.

Holding your rifle high in the air to keep it dry, you plunge into the chilly stream. Your horse is up to the task and soon has you across and on the other side. You are wet and cold, but must continue on your way.

Soon you reach the first group of graders. Here you see the men busily at work removing rocks, filling holes, and smoothing the road bed. It is back-breaking labor. The graders are so far from end o' track that they have a company of soldiers of the United States Army with them to protect them from attack.

Later that day you meet other parties of graders. Some groups are as small as 50 men. Others number as many as 500. From time to time you overtake supply wagons bringing equipment to the graders. Often you meet empty wagons returning to end o' track for more materials. Soon you pass the last party of graders and soldiers. From now on you are on your own, for there will be no troops to protect you until you reach the surveyors.

You see a change in the road bed. The graders have not yet smoothed it, but it has been laid out by the engineers. Deep depressions have been filled. Trees have been removed. Cuts have been made through hills and tunnels dug through mountains. Where the land is flat, stakes have been driven into the ground so that the route will be clearly marked. The final grading, however, must still be done.

That night you and your companion must camp alone. Near a stream you find a place which will conceal you from wandering Indians. You gather some wood and start a fire while your companion goes to hunt for game. He returns with fresh buffalo meat. It tastes wonderful after your hard day's journey.

Soon you roll yourselves into your blankets and fall asleep on the chilly ground.

The next morning you push on, always alert for danger. Suddenly you see a lone figure on a distant hill. Soon others join him. They don't seem to be hostile, but you can't take any chances, and you hold your rifles in readiness. As you draw closer, you are relieved to learn that they are not Indians at all. You have reached the surveyors and engineers, the most advanced party of all.

You spur your horses to join them, and once you have identified yourselves, you all laugh. They were suspicious of you, thinking that you were Indians!

When you announce that you have a message, everyone stops work and crowds around to hear. You tell them of the Union Pacific's decision to step up the race with the Central Pacific. A mighty cheer goes up at the news. Within minutes the men are back at work, singing, shouting, and laughing with excitement.

The tents of the camp are lined up in a military manner and everywhere you see stacks of rifles. You are told that there are 22 men in the surveying party, including teamsters and herders, for there are many animals with the group. And here, the soldiers on guard number a full company.

Early the next morning you prepare to leave. The men return to work. Soldiers stand guard all around. You are just about to mount your horse, when you hear the blood-curdling shriek of an Indian war cry.

Immediately each man seizes a rifle and runs for cover, seeking what little protection a tent or a wagon wheel will provide. Within minutes the Indians are upon you.

From behind a wagon wheel you see the shrieking red men on horseback wildly circling the camp. As rifles crackle, the crisp morning air is filled with the smoke of gunfire and with flying arrows. You and the others shoot back. Constantly moving as they are, the Indians are hard to hit. You just shoot in their direction instead of aiming carefully. Even so, some are hit.

Almost as switfly as it began, the Indian raid is over.

Immediately the men return to work, rifles stacked in preparation for another attack. The soldiers look over the wounded, and you are glad to learn that no one was killed or seriously injured. Next time it could be different.

The captain tells you to get going fast, for this is actually the safest moment. The Indians, busy tending their wounded, are not likely to chase someone leaving the camp.

In a moment you are on your horse and on

your way, and the next day you are once again at end o' track.

Soon you are back at work, and hard work it is. Back and forth you go with water. You must be careful with it as every precious drop has to be brought by train. Indeed, there is little for any purpose other than drinking and cooking. The only chance you and the men have to bathe or wash is when you pass a river. At other times you simply remain dirty. As you perspire, the hot dust cakes on you.

Most of the men do not mind. Many are battle-toughened veterans of the Civil War and are accustomed to rough living. A few are Negroes who not long ago were slaves. Many are Irishmen who have come to America to escape the poverty and hunger of the Old World. Most of them are accustomed to a difficult life.

Even the frequent Indian attacks do not bother them. Work stops until the attackers are beaten off and then continues as though nothing unusual has happened. Every night you go to sleep weary and tired, only to arise early and begin again.

But you are happy and so is everyone else. The exciting race with the Central Pacific keeps everyone working hard. It is very important to all of you for the Union Pacific to lay the most track, for there is a great deal of money at stake. The government will pay each railroad between $16,000 and $48,000 for each mile of track they lay. The lower figure is paid for construction in level areas, and higher amounts for difficult mountainous country. Each company will get 12,800 acres of land alongside of each mile of railroad it builds.

More and more men pour into end o' track, increasing the size of the working crews. The working day becomes longer, lasting from dawn till dusk.

Every Saturday night you all go back to the newest "Hell on Wheels" town for your pay. About every sixty days another town springs up wherever the Union Pacific moves its headquarters and warehouses. Most of these towns disappear just as quickly when the headquarters moves on.

Drinking and gambling are the rule. As most of the men are armed, many an argument is settled with guns. Each weekend the new town's cemetery grows larger. When work begins again on Monday morning, few men have much money left.

Day by day the track moves west. At first, one mile a day was considered fast. As the pace grew more furious, two miles a day were not uncommon. Soon three miles a day, then four and five were being laid. Now, over six miles a day is the usual rate.

Before long the hot, burning days of summer give way to the cooler days of autumn. Then follows the short days and bitter cold of winter. Every morning you must break the ice at the top of the barrel before you can get your water. When you are near a river, the men are so eager for their rare baths they even break through the ice and plunge into the freezing waters.

As the Union Pacific reaches the foothills of the Wasatch Mountains on the border of Wyoming and Utah, you are caught in blizzards. In other years construction stopped for the winter. But now the Central Pacific is coming too close and you must continue. Frequently huge snow drifts must be plowed through to get down to the road bed. Often track is laid right on a bed of snow and ice.

The graders frequently have gone around small hills rather than take the time to cut through them. Now the railroad, instead of going straight, begins to zig-zag over the landscape.

Soon it is early 1869. You are astounded to learn that your crew has laid six and one-half miles of track in a single day. You think this record can never be equalled. But soon this feat is not only equalled, but surpassed. Your crew completes the amazing distance of eight and a half miles in a day.

Meanwhile the Central Pacific, in working across mountains, isn't even waiting to dig tunnels. They are hauling supplies right over the mountain to continue track-laying, leaving the tunnels to be completed afterward.

Also, the Central Pacific is employing more and more Chinese men to increase the large numbers of men already working on the railroad.

It is April, 1869. As winter gives way to spring, plans are made for the tracks to meet at Promontory Point near Ogden, Utah.

The Union Pacific's track-laying record of eight and a half miles in one day still stands, and with only 25 miles to go it seems the Central can't beat it. But suddenly a challenge is received. The Central Pacific is going to try to break the record. You cheer when you hear that your railroad has wagered $10,000 that it can't be done.

The next day your supervisors leave for the Central's work camp to witness the attempt. That evening you get the results. Central has won. They have laid ten miles in a single eighteen-hour day!

The Central Pacific may have won the bet, but you console yourself with knowledge that they did it only after a great deal of special effort. Union Pacific's records were all achieved in the course of ordinary working days.

All construction ceases when the tracks are one rail length apart. The two final rails will be laid at a great historic ceremony celebrating the linking of the entire continent of North America. Not only are you, the crews, and visitors excited, but the entire nation is eagerly awaiting the event. Since the telegraph lines have kept pace with the railroads, the whole country will know the exact moment the last spike is in place.

It is May 10, 1869, the day set for the ceremony. In great excitement you watch the arrival of train after train from both east and west. The brightly decorated coaches are filled with invited guests. Everywhere there are important people: government officials, executives of both railroads, and Army officers. The 21st Military Band is on hand to provide the music.

The big moment arrives. Two locomotives move up, facing each other across the open track. An official of each railroad sets the final, specially made tie in place. A silver plate in the center reads, "The last tie laid on the completion of the Pacific Railroad, May 10, 1869."

Now six Central Pacific men leap forward, and amid tremendous cheering, lay the last two rails.

After a few short speeches and a prayer, there remains only the driving of the four last spikes. Many important guests are invited to help. Soon the two spikes of silver, and the one of mixed silver and gold are in place. One spike remains, this one made of solid gold.

Telegraph operators are busy flashing every detail to the waiting nation. Photographers are taking pictures. To Leland Stanford, Governor of California and one of the Central Pacific's founders, goes the honor of driving the golden spike. Bang goes his sledgehammer.

"Done," is heard on telegraphs everywhere. You and the entire crowd go wild with excitement. The two engines move forward until they touch. The train engineers pour champagne on each other's locomotives, and the band plays a stirring tune. Celebrations and cheering break out all over the United States. Church bells ring. Cannons are shot off. Everywhere there are parades.

North America is now linked by a band of rails from east to west, from the Atlantic to the Pacific, and you have had a part in making this dream come true.

GLOSSARY

Boarding Train — A special train at end o' track that had cars for eating and sleeping.

Central Pacific — The name of the railroad company formed to build the transcontinental railroad from California eastward.

Chairs — Iron supports that are set on the ties to hold the rails in place.

End o' Track — The farthest place the tracks had reached.

Engineers and Surveyors — The men who planned and marked the road bed.

Graders — The men who made the road bed smooth and flat for the tracks that would be laid.

Gauging — Measuring and placing the rails the proper distance apart.

Hell on Wheels — The nickname given to the headquarters towns that sprang up along the railroad.

Omaha, Nebraska — The city at which the Union Pacific started to build its railroad westward.

Prairie — The flat, treeless country across which much of the Union Pacific Railroad was built.

Promontory Point, Utah — The place at which the Union Pacific and Central Pacific rails met.

Siding — A second track which runs beside the main track to permit trains to pass each other.

Spikes — The long iron nails which are driven into the ties to fasten the chairs and rails.

Surveyors — See engineers and surveyors.

Ties — The wooden supports to which the rails are fastened.

Union Pacific — The name of the railroad company formed to build the transcontinental tracks from Omaha, Nebraska, westward.

OTHER LET'S GO BOOKS

Let's Go
- To an Airport
- To an Art Museum
- To an Automobile Factory
- To a Bakery
- To a Ballet
- To Watch a Building Go Up
- To a Candy Factory
- To the Capitol
- To a Circus
- To a City Hall
- To a Clothing Factory
- To Colonial Williamsburg
- To a Concert
- To a Court
- To a Dairy
- To a Dentist
- To a Farm
- To the FBI
- To a Firehouse
- To the First Independence Day
- To a Freight Yard
- To a Garage
- To a Harbor
- To a Hospital
- To the Library
- Logging

Let's Go
- Down the Mississippi with La Salle
- To Mount Vernon
- To a National Park
- For a Nature Walk
- To a Newspaper
- To an Oil Refinery
- To a Planetarium
- To a Police Station
- To a Post Office
- To a Rocket Base
- To a Rubber Plant
- To a Sanitation Department
- To a School
- To a Steel Mill
- To a Supermarket
- To the Supreme Court
- To the Telephone Company
- To a Television Station
- To the United Nations Headquarters
- To the U. S. Mint
- To the United States Air Force Academy
- To Vote
- To a Weather Station
- To West Point
- To the White House
- To a Zoo